Verses From South Yorkshire

Edited by Claire Tupholme

First published in Great Britain in 2007 by:
Young Writers
Remus House
Coltsfoot Drive
Peterborough
PE2 9JX
Telephone: 01733 890066
Website: www.youngwriters.co.uk

SB ISBN 978-1 84602 974 5

Foreword

Young Writers was established in 1991 and has been passionately devoted to the promotion of reading and writing in children and young adults ever since. The quest continues today. Young Writers remains as committed to the nurturing of poetic and literary talent as ever.

This year's Young Writers competition has proven as vibrant and dynamic as ever and we are delighted to present a showcase of the best poetry from across the UK and in some cases overseas. Each poem has been selected from a wealth of *Little Laureates* entries before ultimately being published in this, our sixteenth primary school poetry series.

Once again, we have been supremely impressed by the overall quality of the entries we have received. The imagination, energy and creativity which has gone into each young writer's entry made choosing the poems a challenging and often difficult but ultimately hugely rewarding task - the general high standard of the work submitted ensured this opportunity to bring their poetry to a larger appreciative audience.

We sincerely hope you are pleased with this final collection and that you will enjoy *Little Laureates Verses From South Yorkshire* for many years to come.

Contents

Mitchell Williams (8)   15
Daniella Jackson (9)   16
Chelsea McKay (9)   16
Natasha Jepson (9)   16
Bethany Churm (9)   17
Lauren Eusman   17
Bethany Foster (9)   17
Dominic Starkey (8)   18
Sophie Ward (9)   18
Ellie-Mae Royal (8)   18
James Blake (8)   19
Sophie Dean (8)   19
Liam Hamilton-Greenwood   19

Athersley North Primary School
Chelsey McNally (11)   20
Nicolle Dudley (11)   20
Mollie Jones-Heaton (11)   21
Amy White (10)   21
Bethany Brooke (10)   22
Jamie Broadhead (10)   22
Joshua Bateman (10)   23
Aaron Cosgrove (10)   23
Hannah Ward (11)   24
Richard Appleby (11)   24
Aiden Parrinder (10)   25
Robert Ward (9)   25
Jessica Wake (9)   26
Daniel Thornton (10)   26

Barnburgh Primary School
Finlay Stinson (8)   27
Cody Foster (8)   27
Heather Callan (11)   28
Tim Heptinstall (10)   28
Mark Nicholas Zamora Harrison (10)   29
Rebecca Vaughan (10)   29
Christopher Edward Gray (11)   30
Warren Trinder (11)   30
Liam Moulton (10)   30
Tom Ryall (10)   31

Hill House St Mary's School

Neena Dugar (9)	69
Safia Khan (8)	70
Amelia Laura Nettleton (8)	71
Joshua Clarke (10)	72
Rowena Eves (9)	72

Holy Rood RC Primary School

Thomas Hale (9)	73
Polly Clark (10)	73
Anna McNicholas (9)	74
Mollie Prentice (10)	74
Amy Bell (10)	75

Rudston Preparatory School

Lydia Athey (9)	75
Oliver Bingham (8)	75
Jordan Falding (9)	76
Umar Farouk (8)	76
Molly Blackburn (8)	76
Alicia Harrison (8)	77
Claudia Longdon (9)	77
Umara Malik (8)	77
Emily Miles (9)	78
Amelia Qaiyum (8)	78
Madhav Padmakumar (9)	78
Olivia Tong (9)	79
Mohammad Hammad Hasain Raza (8)	79
Alice Swann (9)	79
Lawrence Hancock (9)	80
Dominic Walsham (8)	80
Nicole Vasey (9)	80
Paige Gibbons (8)	81

Sandringham Primary School

Sandy Ireland (10)	81
Shannon Hughes (11)	82
Kelly Howe (10)	84
George Gears (10)	86
Dominic Farrow (10)	88

The Poems

Desert

The desert, the desert,
An extremely hot desert,
It is so interesting,
It could lead you to sing,
You might even find something!
The desert, the desert.

A camel, a camel,
A dromedary camel,
If a camel comes to tea,
Be sure the toilet is clean,
Because the camel will go there to pee!
A camel, a camel.

A cactus, a cactus,
A very prickly cactus,
It has thorns so sharp,
It could hurt a shark,
You'd better find a cart!
A cactus, a cactus.

Tanvi Khetan (10)

A Metaphor Poem

A full moon is a hot air balloon
Flying around Earth's atmosphere,
A full moon is a target
Waiting to be hit in Heaven's archery range,
A full moon is a football
Waiting to be kicked in the goal of night-time,
A full moon is a cheese
Waiting to be served with crackers,
A full moon is a crystal ball
Waiting to be read.

Alexander Raynes (11)
Anston Hillcrest Primary School

The Moon

A full moon is a beach ball
Floating higher than the fluffy white clouds,
A full moon is a target
Getting to Earth every night,
A full moon is an orange
The ripest, juiciest orange ever,
A full moon is a light
Guiding the way at night,
A full moon is a spinning top
That spins around the sun.

Lauren Smith (10)
Anston Hillcrest Primary School

A Metaphor Poem

A full moon is a ball
Bouncing high over the garden fence,
A full moon is a balloon
Floating high in the midnight sky,
A full moon is a target
Waiting to be hit,
A full moon is an apple
A juicy green apple,
A full moon is a rock
Covered in snow,
A full moon is chocolate
Tasty white chocolate.

Eve Kelly (11)
Anston Hillcrest Primary School

A Metaphor Poem

A full moon is a ball
Bouncing high over the garden fence,
A full moon is a block of cheese
In the high, dark midnight sky,
A full moon is a dartboard in space
That is waiting to be hit,
A full moon is a melon
Flying into the night sky,
A full moon is a ball of cotton
Getting chased by a cat,
A full moon is a basketball
That flew straight into the high hoop.

Emily Richardson (11)
Anston Hillcrest Primary School

Moon Poem

A full moon is a balloon
Floating to the ceiling of the Earth,
A full moon is a target
On God's target range,
A full moon is a fruit
Sitting in the Milky Way's fruit bowl,
A full moon is a ghost's face
Haunting the Earth,
A full moon is a satellite
Orbiting the Earth.

Sam Barke (11)
Anston Hillcrest Primary School

A Metaphor Poem

A full moon is a ball
Bouncing high over the garden fence,
A full moon is a balloon
Floating high up in the galaxy,
A full moon is a target
For the sun to reflect its light,
A full moon is a fruit
That you can almost taste with your taste buds,
A full moon is a cheesy ball
Waiting to be eaten,
A full moon is a Jaffa Cake
Floating high in the Milky Way.

Chloe Cregan (10)
Anston Hillcrest Primary School

The Moon

A new moon is a hook
Hanging from a long fishing rod,
A new moon is a boat
Sailing up in the sea of the stars,
A new moon is a smile
That has fallen from the sun,
A new moon is a dog
Chasing its own tail.

Jack Clare (11)
Anston Hillcrest Primary School

A Day In The Rainforest

Walking in the rainforest
Bright colours all around.
Birds singing and chirping
What a beautiful sound.
Branches on trees are as tall as sky high
Everything's so calm, I feel I could fly.

Oh no, there's a snake, he's hunting for me
His long body is coiled round a tree.
I run for my life, him trailing behind
But then I realise, it is a trick of the mind.
So that was my adventurous day
On a rainforest island, as a castaway.

Fay Hemming (11)
Anston Hillcrest Primary School

Rainforest

R avaging rhino
A lligators angry
I guanas
N owhere
F erocious frogs going
O ver
R ainforest from
E lephants back while
S tamping soundlessly
T oday.

Joseph Raynes (9)
Anston Hillcrest Primary School

Treetop Monkeys

Monkeys, monkeys all around
Swinging from trees
Never falling to the ground.

Swinging their tails
To and fro
Always swinging high
Never swinging low.

In this rainforest there can be found
Many, many monkeys all around
So if you should ever visit there
If you play with monkeys
Please *beware!*

Sidonie-Mae Hill (10)
Anston Hillcrest Primary School

The Rainforest

Leaves rustling in the breeze
Tall, slightly slanting trees
Birds, parrots
Flying high
While the sun fades
From the sky.

Snakes, sliding round my feet
Searching for their food (that's meat)
And when that snake then finds its prey
He'll have eaten enough that day.

Hannah Foster (10)
Anston Hillcrest Primary School

Clever Island

Clever Island is the best,
Better than all the rest,
While I'm having fun,
My friends are laid in the sun,
I like to play and run in the sea,
While my friends watch me,
Golden sand I see all day,
As crystal-blue sea shines on me,
You can hear palm trees rustling,
Water falls down as the colourful birds fly by.

Serena Evers (11)
Anston Hillcrest Primary School

A Metaphor Poem

A full moon is a hot air balloon
Floating slowly but silently into space,
A full moon is a target
Tensely waiting to be shot,
A full moon is a juicy orange
Lying in a colourful fruit bowl,
A full moon is a biscuit
That hasn't been eaten,
A full moon is a snowball
Flying through the air.

Mae Brooksbank (11)
Anston Hillcrest Primary School

Rainforest - Cinquains

High trees
Massive smooth leaves
Animals all around
The parrots make a lovely sound
Jungle

Wet ground
Rain hard, but soft
Rainbow-coloured flowers
Poisonous snakes finding their lunch
Coiling.

Imogen Stewart (11)
Anston Hillcrest Primary School

The Rainforest

Frogs leaping tree to tree,
Anaconda eyeing me.
Crocodile like a log,
In the mud a snorting hog.
Lizards catching flies all day,
Monkeys want to climb and play.
Toucans pinching fruit from me,
That anaconda's still there I see.
Well, I'd better go away,
Before I'm an anaconda meal today.

Andrew Hemming (11)
Anston Hillcrest Primary School

The Rainforest

Exotic flowers small and stubby
Scaly lizards shining in the sun
Bumblebees searching for honey
Where's my lunch? I want some!

Waving through the jungle trees
Up in the sky fluttering butterflies
There's a very warm feeling in the breeze
Although it's very slimy and damp.

Colourful birds flying sky-high
Snakes are twisting around trees
You're excited, so am I
And lots of lovely shaded leaves.

Nancy Leitch (10)
Anston Hillcrest Primary School

Deep In The Rainforest

Animals all around,
Making a beautiful sound,
Insects walking,
Parrots talking,
Snakes coiling,
The weather's boiling,
Here we go again,
Into the leopard's den.

Danielle Horton (10)
Anston Hillcrest Primary School

Exploring The Rainforest

Exotic flowers in the breeze,
When the monkeys start to tease,
Scaly lizards crawling by,
The birds are chirping, flying sky-high,
Warm but shaded,
The sun's almost faded.

Victoria Burgin (9)
Anston Hillcrest Primary School

The Rainforest

Leaves rustling in the breeze
With tall, swaying, slanting trees . . .
Birds, parrots and eagles fly
While penguins go proudly marching by.

Monkeys, monkeys all around
Swinging from trees without a sound
Snakes, snakes sliding down
Sliding down with a little frown.

Sasha Niamh Yates (9)
Anston Hillcrest Primary School

Nature's Shield

Crawling, eating,
Never stops growing.
Hiding, defending,
A rock-solid shell.
Emerging from the fortress,
Bringing out the treasure,
That holds a second life.

Jack Holcombe (10)
Anston Hillcrest Primary School

Sounds Of The Jungle

Monkeys, monkeys swinging through the jungle,
Birds cheeping, what a lovely sound,
Leaves rustling, snakes hissing,
Watch out!
Butterflies everywhere
Parrots flying all about,
Listen - hear the song of the river
And hear the wind whistling.

Bethany Waller (10)
Anston Hillcrest Primary School

Animals In The Rainforest

I can see a snake waiting for his prey,
I can hear birds - their sweet sounds,
I can touch the tree, it feels bumpy,
I can taste the air so humid,
I can smell the flowers so sweet.

Robert Boulton (11)
Anston Hillcrest Primary School

The Enchanting Rainforest

Rain in the rainforest
Sand near the sea
The leaves on the trees
Rustling all around me.

The birds up so high
The sand so low
But in the middle
There is nothing to flow . . .

Megan Kelly (9)
Anston Hillcrest Primary School

I Explored

I explored
I explored the forest
I explored the forest dense, high
I explored the forest dense, high and low
I explored the forest dense, high and low, which holds
I explored the forest dense, high and low, which holds the key
to destiny.

Toby Wildgoose (9)
Anston Hillcrest Primary School

Love

Love sounds like happiness in your ears
Love tastes like strawberries
Love smells like perfume
Love looks like roses floating in the air
Love feels like shivers down your spine
Love reminds you of flowers.

Abbey Freeman (9)
Aston Lodge Primary School

Love

Love reminds me of that one kiss
Love looks red like fire
Love smells like roses
Love tastes like sugar.

Charlie Green (8)
Aston Lodge Primary School

Love

It sounds like peace
It tastes like flowers
It smells like strawberries floating in a stream
It looks beautiful
It feels like when I first kissed
It reminds me of when I was born
It makes me forget all the bad things
Like when I had a fight
It makes me think of summertime.

Kadie Senior (9)
Aston Lodge Primary School

Love

Love sounds like a wedding
Love tastes like a mini strawberry
Love smells like a red rose growing in your garden
Love looks like the sky
Love feels nervous
Love reminds you of pink flowers.

Liam Wragg (8)
Aston Lodge Primary School

Love

Love sounds like birds singing
Love tastes like smooth strawberries
Love smells like the scent of roses
Love looks like a heart full of pink and feelings for another
Love feels beautiful
Love reminds me of a bunch of roses.

Paige Bland (9)
Aston Lodge Primary School

Love

Love is the colour pink like rosy cheeks
Love sounds like romantic music as quiet as a mouse
Love tastes like a chocolate bar
Love smells like roses in the sky
Love looks like a bright red heart
Love feels like a furry dog
Love reminds me of a hug.

Charlotte Staniland (9)
Aston Lodge Primary School

Love

Love sounds like music flowing through the sky
Love tastes like love is coming back to life
Love smells like a rose air freshener all over
Love looks like the love heart
Starts from black and turns red
To a glittery, reddy pink
Love feels like your heart has turned to a love heart
Love reminds you of the day your mum and dad got married.

Keeran Thompson
Aston Lodge Primary School

Love

It sounds like a mouse
It feels like cherries
It smells like chocolate
It reminds you of apples
It looks like roses
Its taste is like a church.

Abigail Smith (8)
Aston Lodge Primary School

Love

Love sounds like wind waving in the air
Love tastes like strawberries with melted chocolate
Love smells like flowers floating in the sky
Love looks like dolphins jumping to kiss
Love feels like a couple kissing in the garden
Love reminds me of roses in a flock of red
Love is pink to make boys wink.

Chloe Williamson (9)
Aston Lodge Primary School

Love

Love sounds like birds tweeting in the sky
Love tastes like roses in the air
Love smells like daffodils
Love looks like chocolate
Love feels like a bath
Love reminds me of beautiful eyes.

Connor Hunt (9)
Aston Lodge Primary School

Love

It sounds like a rose in the air
It tastes like strawberries
It smells like bubble bath
It looks like petals growing
It feels like a kiss
It reminds me of a kiss.

Mitchell Williams (8)
Aston Lodge Primary School

Love

Love sounds like birds tweeting in my ear
Love tastes like chocolate made by angels from up above
Love smells like roses
Love looks like two doves flying in front of me
Love feels like butterflies in my tummy
Love reminds me of happiness all around the world.

Daniella Jackson (9)
Aston Lodge Primary School

Love

Love is the colour red
As red as your cheeks
Love smells like a garden full of roses
Love sounds like birds humming in the sky
It reminds you of a kiss once upon a dream
It feels like cuddling a teddy bear
It looks like a heart beating in front of you.

Chelsea McKay (9)
Aston Lodge Primary School

Love

Love sounds like birds whistling
Love looks like Americans listening
Love feels like cold, freezing water
Love reminds me of a present he has bought her
Love smells like the pollen of a rose
Love is like a person on their very tippy-toes.

Natasha Jepson (9)
Aston Lodge Primary School

Love

Love feels like someone laying roses around me
Love sounds like the birds tweeting
Love tastes like strawberries covered in chocolate stars
Love smells like fresh flowers
Love looks like the grass swaying from side to side
Love reminds me of a breeze just blowing at me.

Bethany Churm (9)
Aston Lodge Primary School

Love

Love smells like strawberries
Love feels like stars in your stomach
Love tastes like roses
Love sounds like birds
Love reminds you of roses
Love looks like butterflies.

Lauren Eusman
Aston Lodge Primary School

Love

Love feels like a rose
Love sounds like an anniversary
Love tastes like a cherry
Love smells like a rose
Love looks like an angel in the sky
Love reminds me of a flowing river.

Bethany Foster (9)
Aston Lodge Primary School

Love

Love sounds like peaceful music
Love tastes like cherries
Love smells like the fresh air in the morning
Love looks like a sweet rose
Love feels like a soothing bath
Love reminds me of a cute baby.

Dominic Starkey (8)
Aston Lodge Primary School

Love

Love smells like chocolate
Love feels like water going down the river softly
Love sounds like birds singing sweetly
Love looks like roses
Love tastes like strawberries
Love reminds you of the one you love
Love is in the air.

Sophie Ward (9)
Aston Lodge Primary School

Love

Love is in the air
Love smells like sweet red roses
Love tastes like sweet strawberries
Love feels like a soft piece of grass
Love reminds me of chocolate
Love looks like an angelfish.

Ellie-Mae Royal (8)
Aston Lodge Primary School

Love

Love is as big as the universe,
Or it could be as small as a nail,
It looks like a bunch of flowers as big as a doorway!
And smells as sweet as honey!

It could be as blue as the sky,
Or it could be very high!
It tastes like strawberries as sweet as roses
And is as soft as a cushion.

Make it as yellow as the sun,
But no, it's as blue as the sky.
I'm going to have a trick put on me,
I'll be as small as a pie!

James Blake (8)
Aston Lodge Primary School

Love

Love feels like a furry teddy bear hugging you till you're warm
Love sounds like the music in a fancy restaurant
Love tastes like chocolates running down your throat
Love looks like a heart running after you
Love smells like your first ever lipstick
Love reminds you of a kiss on the cheek
Love is the colour red, as red as strawberries.

Sophie Dean (8)
Aston Lodge Primary School

Love

It feels like a soft pillow
It sounds like love in the air
It tastes like lollipops
It smells like soap
It looks like a love heart.

Liam Hamilton-Greenwood
Aston Lodge Primary School

School

School, school what do you do?
Using paper with sticky glue,
Listening to the teacher all day,
Ready for when we do our SATs in May.

English is boring,
Maths is good,
Science is difficult,
I wish I understood.

My behaviour might be bad
And my teacher will be mad,
I'll write her a letter,
Promising her I will be better.

Chelsey McNally (11)
Athersley North Primary School

Best Mates!

My best made is Donnie,
She's got a friend called Annie,
Donnie is cheeky
And very, very sneaky.

Nicky is her best mate,
She lives on the same estate,
Nicky is funny,
They eat lots of honey.

Best mates forever,
Live together, die together,
All the fun we'll have together,
Try to make it last forever.

Nicolle Dudley (11)
Athersley North Primary School

Chocolate

White chocolate, dark chocolate
All the chocolate in the world is lovely,
Is lovely,
Crunchie, Caramel, Milky Way,
Munch, munch, munch
It gets better every day
It's lovely, it's lovely!

Mollie Jones-Heaton (11)
Athersley North Primary School

Pets

Pets are fun,
Pets are great,
Even if they live in a cage.

They depend on you,
To keep them alive.

Teach them tricks,
Brush their fur,
Pick them up
And bath them.

Cuddle them,
Stroke them,
Talk to them
And name them.

Feed your pets,
Give them water,
They depend on you,
To keep them alive.

Amy White (10)
Athersley North Primary School

Snow

Snow is light
He sneaks around showering snow
Freezing people in his way
Causing people to freeze and scare
Making sure there is no one there

When people cry he freezes their tears
Causing them to freeze and peer
Freezing windows so no one can see
Causing people to wonder why

The day is ending very quickly
The man is melting
And so am I.

Bethany Brooke (10)
Athersley North Primary School

Winter

The snow is white
The clouds are grey
Lots of frost can be seen
The snow twinkles in the sun
People skate on the frozen pond
Crunch, crunch, crunch
As you walk along
The children sledge down the hill
All the children are playing out
So very pleasing to the passing eye
The gentle snow touches my face
Children have snowball fights
Isn't the winter a beautiful sight!

Jamie Broadhead (10)
Athersley North Primary School

A Guide Dog

There's this dog
Who doesn't live with me
Near some frogs
His name is Floyd.

He's a guide dog
Who's nearly passed his guide course
With some other dogs
His name is Floyd.

He's a golden retriever
That takes blind people out
Who is a believer
His name is Floyd.

He guides people
That are blind
Round a shop
His name is Floyd.

People with white eyes
Say that they're blind
Floyd's there to guide them
And his name is Floyd.

Joshua Bateman (10)
Athersley North Primary School

The Sky

The sky is blue
Everybody is out
The sun is bright
Trees are waving about
The sky has clouds
They are floating around in the breeze
That makes me wheeze
And then at the end of the day
Everybody sleeps in their bed.

Aaron Cosgrove (10)
Athersley North Primary School

My Grandma

My grandma's name is Jean
She's never ever mean
She likes to bake
She makes the best cakes.

She's very, very pretty
And she's also very witty
Her bedroom is pink
She always winks.

She likes my long, long hair
She always, always cares
In her hair she has a thousand curls
Her favourite chocolate bar is a Twirl.

She's going on holiday to France
To have a little dance
Her husband's name is Trevor
He's not very clever.

That's my grandma!

Hannah Ward (11)
Athersley North Primary School

Things

A mouse goes squeak,
A door goes creak,
A baby falls asleep,
What wonderful things.

A bird takes flight,
A boy flies a kite,
An owl hunts at night,
What wonderful things.

Water goes *splash*,
A hammer goes *bash*,
The cup goes *smash*,
What wonderful things!

Richard Appleby (11)
Athersley North Primary School

World

The sky is blue, the grass is green,
The world is round, only two colours to be seen,
The birds sing, the people chatter,
Nothing changes in this matter,
The sea is blue,
The space is black,
Nothing changes in this matter,
Snow is white, snow is fun
Ice is great
And it is a good day for a snowball fight,
All the colours are fun for my eyes
It is all great in this place.

Aiden Parrinder (10)
Athersley North Primary School

Snow

Snow falls
Snow is white
It is cold
It is soft
It is fun
It melts in the sun
In the night
It snows even more
When it snows
It is deep
Snow's thin
The snow melts
Into water
The snow crackles
Under you feet.

Robert Ward (9)
Athersley North Primary School

Jasmin

I've got a cat called Jasmin,
I love her very much,
She gives me kisses on my nose
And tries to bite my toes.

She plays with toys and makes a noise,
She gives me cuddles and hugs,
She loves to eat and sleep,
She loves to climb and jump.

She is black and white
And kind and nice,
She jumps around and licks my hand,
She goes *miaow, miaow, miaow,* all day long.

Jessica Wake (9)
Athersley North Primary School

DIY

Pass me a hammer
throw me some nails
and I will make some
things for you.

I'll hammer and tap
and bash and bang
and whoop and swoop
and clash and clang.

I'll make a bike
I'll make a bed
I'll make a helmet
for your head.

I'll snap some wood
I'll break some stone
I'll huff and puff
and whine and groan.

Daniel Thornton (10)
Athersley North Primary School

My Adventure As A Penguin

Through the Antarctic night
I walked and walked and walked
I saw seals all huddled up tight
I crept across with fear and fright
Whiskers like wire, spots on their backs
They looked like fish, gigantically fat!
I ran with fright, a shiver down my back
To get over my fright, I dived in the sea, inky black
I caught my first fish, but dropped it down low
I left it alone and made my way back through
The breaking ice, back through the seals
Gigantically fat, I sat down alone, all shivery and cold
I gazed at the moon with a million star friends
Then gazed once again in the pool at my feet
Then I saw my mum's face
It gave me the courage to find my way home
And snuggle up warm with my family at last.

Finlay Stinson (8)
Barnburgh Primary School

Dennis The Menace

Dennis the Menace
He can't play tennis
He runs around the court
Like a big cool menace
He saw Mr Wilson
Having some trouble
Dennis was there
To make it double!

Cody Foster (8)
Barnburgh Primary School

Hedgehog

Prickly, spiky, as sharp as needles
This fence is guarding his soul as a sea of spears
Pink and tight, small and round
A little pink button on his face
Tiny legs scuttle across the ground
As fast as a flash of light
An army always prepared to defend the precious treasure
Fur as soft as a delicate touch
Short and as brown as an animal's coat
Hiding in the leaves like a long-lost toy
Tiny black marbles shimmer in the moonlight.

Heather Callan (11)
Barnburgh Primary School

Airbus A380

A hungry cheetah
Soaring like a monster
An aluminium beast
With its engines roaring like thunderous storms
Feared when heard
A bird of prey
With wings as wide as the sea
Blinding lights blinking in the darkness
Like giant cats' eyes
Above all
A dream liner of the heavens.

Tim Heptinstall (10)
Barnburgh Primary School

What Is It?

It's a box of secrets waiting to be told,
It's a peacock's tail ready to unfold,
It's in a town full of answers and bravery,
It's a great flowing field of sagacity,
It's a gaping hole imprisoning people's thoughts,
It's holding greater words than the mind itself,
Its pages of wisdom spill upon you,
Its silky path leading you to victory,
Its wisdom is never-ending . . .
It's a book here from centuries ago . . .

Mark Nicholas Zamora Harrison (10)
Barnburgh Primary School

Dog

Biting the ground, taking flesh
Racing away, sprinting
Cooling down from the big race
A doorbell ringing, *woof, woof*
Sticks sticking out of the rough ground
Curling wire bending, curling and wagging
Orange juice pouring out of a jug
Yellow hills with disgusting flakes
Another race as they're running away
King of the park
Winning, awaiting being groomed.

Rebecca Vaughan (10)
Barnburgh Primary School

Cave

A mouth swallowing the sea,
A basking shark devouring all,
Hiding place for crabs,
A hollow pizza crust,
Like a black freezing fridge,
A misty cavern full of secrets,
A treasure chest of ancient bones.

Christopher Edward Gray (11)
Barnburgh Primary School

Frozen River

A bright glint on the horizon
A frozen silver gem
A white mirror of the world around it
A cold serpent heading for the shore
An icy prison for water
A glass cover, bright and shiny
Sheets of metal that you can't fall through . . .
Well, mostly at least.

Warren Trinder (11)
Barnburgh Primary School

Torchlight

A fiery laser burning into my eye
An illuminous beam searching for its destiny
A glaring beam of burning heat
A golden eye glaring upon me
A golden blanket covering all it sees
A golden fish gliding on the bottom of the sea.

Liam Moulton (10)
Barnburgh Primary School

Footie

A shooting rocket flying through the air.
A fireball ripping the net open.
A dart hitting bullseye.
An eyeball shooting out of its socket.
The moon curling into the bottom corner of the horizon.
A golf ball putted into the hole.

Tom Ryall (10)
Barnburgh Primary School

Tree

I am Atlas
I hold the might of the ferocious sky
Held in place by many slithering serpents
A security guard protecting my land
A raging, anchored octopus swaying frantically in the wind
Home to thousands of tiny creatures.

Nicholas Short (10)
Barnburgh Primary School

Daisy

Hiding from enemies day and night
The puffy white petals are its light
A pretty little chain
As precious as jewellery
Surround the saviour with its glory.

Jessica Louise Vance (10)
Barnburgh Primary School

A Skyscraper

A large, sharp finger pointing at the sky,
A massive metal mountain,
Stretching high to reach the sparkling stars,
The strong Iron Man,
Shimmering in the warm, golden sun,
A tall, silver giraffe holding creatures within,
A shiny giant,
Head in the clouds,
Feet on the ground,
Countless eyes peering down at their toes,
Watching the world,
Until the day is complete and the lights dim . . .

Amelia Hooper (11)
Barnburgh Primary School

The Tree

A wacky hair day full of insects
Colours full of fruit
A giant waving softly on a windy day to passers-by
A hungry monster's teeth grind through me for paper
My arms reach as far as the stars
I'm locked to the ground.

Dan Waldron (11)
Barnburgh Primary School

The Computer

A magician's box full of tricks
A large slab of white chocolate waiting to be eaten
Tangled spaghetti hanging off a plate
A plain jacket revealing a colourful shirt
Its mouth opens wide, swallowing CDs.

Daniel Lee (11)
Barnburgh Primary School

Ocean

Trespassers beware, a hungry bear is what I may be!
A calm whale, elegantly swallowing
Treasures that need to unfold,
You hunt for what lies beneath me;
Fish, treasure or something else . . . ?
Rainstorms in a sheet of octopuses' arms
Spread across the world
The ocean, a salty cover with a tangy smell, but no pepper!
I protect my family which live inside me!
The Pacific, Atlantic and Indian Ocean too!
At night I lay awake gazing into the shimmering moon's silhouette,
Gleams and beams, the sky is a sea
And is my bed of dreams,
It is glittering and sparkling with fish!

Tegan Lee-Foster (10)
Barnburgh Primary School

Camera

A pulled trigger off a shooting pistol
A picture story waiting to unfold
A winking friend saying hello
A watchful eye
A flashing light ready to catch you
A shooting star-like flashing light.

Emily Jones (10)
Barnburgh Primary School

Seal

Their whiskers like pipe cleaners
All snuggled up tight
Big and small, small and big
Their colours so bright.

Amelia Britten (8)
Barnburgh Primary School

A Strawberry

Hidden behind groups of friends,
A bird's snack during the day,
A main attraction for families,
The ruby you can see for miles,
A soft red heart studded with black specks,
Sweet as sugar and as sour as lemons,
Holding long green hands reaching from within,
A red squashy pillow for insects.

Hannah Teasdale (10)
Barnburgh Primary School

Rose

A proud soldier stands tall guarding the table
Petals as soft as a sheet
Pillows of blood
Heart protected by a satin blanket
As delicate as tissue paper
A sweet cloud of aroma drifting
A secret spy watching a romantic meal.

Atalanta Smith (10)
Barnburgh Primary School

Frogs

F rogs live in water
R eally hard to catch
O utside all the time
G reen and shimmery
S lippery and slimy!

Bethany Pearce (8)
Barnburgh Primary School

The Eye Of The Tiger!

A furious, hungry zebra crossing,
A mouth of yellow daggers,
An orange, heartless beast,
Haunts the island's soul!

A careful listener to any conversation,
Monstrous claws awaiting his opponent,
Teeth grinding through his victim,
Imprisoning the unworthy!

Olivia Ann Harpham (10)
Barnburgh Primary School

My Horse Diamond

My horse Diamond is clear white
She is so shiny
Her eyes are bright green
She lives in a stable
So cosy and cream.

Bethany Eve Kelly (8)
Barnburgh Primary School

Giraffes

G iraffes
 I mpossible to look short
R eally soft
A lways nibbling leaves
F unny
F antastic
E xtremely tall
S trange and wonderful, not silly at all!

Laura Fallon (9)
Barnburgh Primary School

Puppy Paws

P uppy paws, puppy paws
U nstoppable in their affections
P layful, cute, adorable, cuddly
P laying around the lake
I t snuggles up tight in its basket at night
E very time in the morning it gives me a bright and early warning
S imply silly, simply good, but I like them just the way they are.

Ellie-Nicole Foster (9)
Barnburgh Primary School

A Polar Bear

I am a polar bear running in the snow
I love fish and I am white with a great height
But be careful because you will have a fright
I might *bite!*
Bite, bite, bite, bite!

Susannah Willis (9)
Barnburgh Primary School

A Snowman

I am a little snowman sitting in the snow
I live on the frost, I live down the road
If you ever get too warm
I'll give you a frosty delight
And you'll love me forever
Even through the night
I never get too warm
I always am cold, cold, cold.

Megan Maloney (9)
Barnburgh Primary School

Rabbits

They are grey, they're small,
They're fluffy and more,
They live in a hut,
Cosy and warm,
They nibble on carrots,
They love dandelion leaves,
Rabbits are the best,
My favourite pets.

Chloe Moulton (8)
Barnburgh Primary School

Chocolate

I love chocolate
It tastes lovely
It's sweet and rich
It melts in your mouth
And slips down your throat
I like the colour
White chocolate, dark chocolate
And light brown.

Lauren Tordoff (8)
Barnburgh Primary School

A Little Red Robin

A little red robin
Sat upon a tree
Here comes a cat
He is going to eat me
He is going to eat me
With his jaws
And crush me
With his claws
Here comes the cat!

Michael Barton (9)
Barnburgh Primary School

Dogs

Dogs are dirty, smelly and not very clean
Always jumping for a treat
Like humans, they're always eager to eat
Dogs are just the same, except they walk on four feet
Dogs are very friendly and faithful
And they're very good friends.

Jack Tordoff (9)
Barnburgh Primary School

Dogs

D ogs are cute and cuddly, messy and wet
O oh, where are my slippers in red
G osh! He's got my slippers in red
S illy dog, you shouldn't eat slippers!

William Naylor (9)
Barnburgh Primary School

Spring

S nowdrops start it
P rimroses continue
R ed spring pansies
I n my
N eighbours'
G ardens.

Anna-Mae Meakin (8)
Barnburgh Primary School

A Girl At School

There once was a girl in school
She didn't go by the rules
That girl, she slept on a mat
Just like Poppy, her cat
She was not very cool.

Everyone thought she was a fool
She liked going to the pool
She had red hair
And everybody stared
She always wore a jewel.

When she was playing hide-and-seek
She always used to peek
She always drew her hens
With her gel pens
And when she squeaked
She made a funny noise, *eek!*

Courtney Temple (8)
Barnburgh Primary School

Dogs

Dogs are dirty, smelly and sometimes clean
Always jumping, looking for a treat
Dogs like to walk all the time
But they do not really like water.

Andrew Trinder (9)
Barnburgh Primary School

A Boy At School

There once was a boy in school
He always wanted to rule
He had multicoloured hair
Everyone did stare
They were very cruel.

They didn't think it was fair
That he had multicoloured hair
They asked their mums
Who smacked their bums
And sat them on the chair.

He dyed his hair
But said it wasn't fair
He wore a hat
With a big black sack
He looked like a bear!

Joshua William Teasdale (7)
Barnburgh Primary School

My Pen

Miss, my pen has run out
It ran out and gave a shout
It came back in with a big grin
And hopped into the bin
'Stop shouting out'
Miss gave a shout.

Brooke Shayler (7)
Barnburgh Primary School

The Boy In School

There once was a boy in school
He was very cool
His name was Jack
Once he broke his back
Sometimes he tried to be a fool.

He liked to rule
And swim in a pool
He got a rack
And ate a snack
He crash-landed in the pool.

He survived crash-landing
In the pool
But felt a bit
Of a fool.

Sam Jones (7)
Barnburgh Primary School

Funny Poem

There once was a boy in school
Who always obeyed the rule
He always was very good
He never played in the mud
But sometimes was very cruel.

He had purple hair
Everybody stared
He was very fat
Like a bat
But he didn't care.

Daniel Procter (7)
Barnburgh Primary School

The Open Door

(Based on 'The Door' by Miroslav Holub)

Go and open the door
Maybe there's a bear playing in the forest
His lovely brown fur glistening in the sun.

Maybe there are trees
With blue trunks and yellow leaves.

Maybe there is a black bat
Flying in the air.

Maybe there's some leaves
Falling from the sky.

Connor Skelton (8)
Beck Primary School

The Open Door

(Based on 'The Door' by Miroslav Holub)

Go and open the door,
Maybe there is
An invisible monster
Scaring a man.

Maybe there are
Spiders spinning
Cotton cobwebs.

Maybe there are
Ants in there
Climbing up legs and biting people.

Maybe there are
Loads of creatures
That will eat you!

Mathew Cattermole (8)
Beck Primary School

The Open Door

(Based on 'The Door' by Miroslav Holub)

Go and open the door
Maybe outside there's an ocean
In the daylight in summer.

Maybe there is a noise
From a dolphin.

Maybe there's a blanket
Of crystal-blue water.

Maybe there's a seagull
Chasing grey swimming fish.

Maybe there's a great white shark
Searching with its jaws to kill.

Daniel Hempshall (8)
Beck Primary School

The Open Door

(Based on 'The Door' by Miroslav Holub)

Go and open the door
Maybe there's a clown
Eating fire.

Maybe there's a grey slimy fish
Marching down the road.

Maybe there's a black cat
Flying beside an aeroplane.

Maybe there are four ostriches
Walking upside down.

Maybe there's a giant flea
Playing football.

Joe Beal (9)
Beck Primary School

The Open Door

(Based on 'The Door' by Miroslav Holub)

Go and open the door
Maybe there is a toilet with legs
Walking around the school

Maybe there is a mouse in a house
Playing on a PSP
The game is 'Need for Speed Underground 2'

Maybe there is a dragon
Playing hockey
With a rhino

Maybe there is a caterpillar
Having a fight
With a butterfly

Brandon Hicks (8)
Beck Primary School

Open The Door

(Based on 'The Door' by Miroslav Holub)

Go and open the door
Maybe there is a talking car
Driving on the road
Maybe there is a flying boat
Maybe there is a walking tree
Or maybe there is a talking house.

Chloe Idel (7)
Beck Primary School

The Open Door
(Based on 'The Door' by Miroslav Holub)

Go and open the door
Maybe there is a massive grey seal
In dungarees, ready for a disco.

Maybe there is a sparkling, shiny key
Like ten pieces of gold.

Maybe there is a pink lion
Riding a new bike.

Maybe there is a glass TV
Getting ready to teach a class.

Maybe there is a massive carrot
Eating a human being.

Maybe there is a red potato
Wearing a Sheffield United kit.

Katie Flanagan (9)
Beck Primary School

The Open Door
(Based on 'The Door' by Miroslav Holub)

Go and open the door
Maybe there's a river
That's made from shiny gold.

Maybe there's a giant monster
That delivers chocolate.

Maybe some sort of dogs
Rule humans.

Carl Armstrong (8)
Beck Primary School

The Open Door

(Based on 'The Door' by Miroslav Holub)

Maybe behind the door
There is a pink rabbit with bling

There is a Subaru Impretza

Maybe there is a mansion
And a Rolls Royce
Just for me

There is a beaver
Playing ice hockey
Using his tail as a stick.

Charlie Whiteley (8)
Beck Primary School

The Open Door

(Based on 'The Door' by Miroslav Holub)

Go and open the door
There might be a teacher
Teaching a class

Go and open the door
There might be a sports car
Driving around.

Go and open the door
There might be a Dalmatian
Barking.

Kane Taylor (8)
Beck Primary School

The Open Door

(Based on 'The Door' by Miroslav Holub)

Go and open the door
Maybe there is a ghost whistling,

Maybe there is a funky stereo
Dancing to his favourite tune,

Maybe there is a ghost
Coming as he whistles,

Maybe there is a lamp
Flickering itself on and off,

Maybe there is a five-legged dog
Prancing on the moon.

Abby Turner (8)
Beck Primary School

The Open Door

(Based on 'The Door' by Miroslav Holub)

Go and open the door,
Maybe there is a snake,
Wearing bling.

Maybe there is a sparkling,
Colourful rainbow,
With a pot of gold at the end.

Maybe there is a blue shark,
Spiking up his hair with gel.

Maybe there is a tyrannosaurus,
Singing to a cloud,
To make it go to sleep.

Maybe there is a bogey monster,
Singing 'Twinkle, Twinkle, Little Star'.

Alex Westney (8)
Beck Primary School

The Open Door

(Based on 'The Door' by Miroslav Holub)

Go and open the door
Maybe there is a dinosaur
With a black suit on.

Maybe there is a snake
Wearing bling
Ready to go to a nightclub with his friends.

Maybe there is a shark
Eating muck off dirty plates
That no one has scrubbed for years.

Anees Botham (9)
Beck Primary School

The Open Door

(Based on 'The Door' by Miroslav Holub)

Go and open the door
Maybe there is a glistening unicorn
Storming up the street.

Maybe there is a Terminator
Killing people.

Maybe there is a three-headed dog
Jumping up and down.

Maybe there is a vampire
Dying in a cupboard.

Maybe there is a rat
Tap dancing.

Maybe there is a rat
Shouting at a snake.

Brendan Menday (8)
Beck Primary School

A Poem To Be Spoken Silently

(Based on 'A Poem to be Spoken Silently' by Pie Corbett)

It was so calm
That I heard the leaves rustling
In the whirling wind.

It was so still
That I heard a tiny, lovely mouse
Playing softly on the keyboard
In an old abandoned house.

It was so silent
That I heard the full blue moon
Move from the clouds.

It was so quiet
That I heard a beautiful ladybug moving
In the wavy grass.

It was so quiet
That I heard the magical street lights
Go off.

It was so still
That I heard a pig-eared dog
Wishing it had fins.

It was so calm
That I heard a cat singing opera
For someone.

It was so silent
That I heard a rabbit
Brush its fur.

It was so silent
That I heard a frog
Crouch softly.

Abigail Carlton (8)
Beck Primary School

A Poem To Be Spoken Silently

(Based on 'A Poem to be Spoken Silently' by Pie Corbett)

It was so quiet
That I could hear a leaf crackle under my feet
As I tiptoed about.

It was so calm
That I could hear the flower petals unfurling
Like a sprinkle of glitter, drifting towards me.

It was so peaceful
That I could hear the sun use its magical powers
To control its shine.

It was so still
That I could hear the wind
Only speak the tiniest whisper.

I was so quiet
That I could hear the tide
Rolling in from the sea
Over from a far country.

Whitney Finn (8)
Beck Primary School

The Open Door

(Based on 'The Door' by Miroslav Holub)

Maybe there is a ghost whistling
Maybe there is a ghost telling a story
Maybe there is a man wishing for a mouse
Maybe there is a man shivering down the stairs
Maybe there is a spider making its web
Maybe there is a rabbit eating a pig.

Brandan Jones (9)
Beck Primary School

A Poem To Be Spoken Silently

(Based on 'A Poem to be Spoken Silently' by Pie Corbett)

It was so quiet
That I heard the radiator whistling at me
Like it was trying to talk to me.

It was so still
That I heard a fire next door crackle
Like crackling fireworks.

It was so peaceful
That I heard a hair falling to the floor
Like a leaf being blown around.

It was so quiet
That I heard the grass swishing
Like mud blowing around.

It was so still
That I heard the rain falling on the grass
Like mud falling to the ground.

Ricki Bradford (8)
Beck Primary School

A Poem To Be Spoken Silently

(Based on 'A Poem to be Spoken Silently' by Pie Corbett)

It was so quiet
That I heard birds singing.

It was so peaceful
I heard my eyes blinking.

It was so still
That I heard the trees blowing.

It was so calm
That I heard red cats being scary.

Awlia Ali Magan (8)
Beck Primary School

A Poem To Be Spoken Silently

(Based on 'A Poem to be Spoken Silently' by Pie Corbett)

It was so quiet
That I heard a spider crawling up my big, shiny wall.

It was so peaceful
That I heard a very sleepy owl.

It was so still
That I heard a breeze from the bright, shiny window.

It was so silent
That I heard some strange noise in the middle of the night.

Bethan Prosser (8)
Beck Primary School

A Poem To Be Spoken Silently

(Based on 'A Poem to be Spoken Silently' by Pie Corbett)

It was so quiet
That I could hear the flowers growing
In the garden.

It was so calm
That I could hear an ant creeping
Through the fresh grass in the summer.

It was so silent
That I could hear the world spinning around
Like a roundabout.

It was so quiet
That I could hear the clouds floating in the air
Like the moon and stars are doing.

Tia Langton (8)
Beck Primary School

A Poem To Be Spoken Silently

(Based on 'A Poem to be Spoken Silently' by Pie Corbett)

It was so quiet
That I heard a hair falling to the floor
Like a mouse running across the floor.

It was so still
That I heard a cloud fly away
In the blue sky like a bird in the air.

It was so peaceful
That I heard a watch ticking
Like a rocket in the air.

It was so calm
That I heard a wolf creeping
In the woods.

It was so quiet
That I heard rain falling on the grass
Like a drum.

Ellen Lee (9)
Beck Primary School

A Poem To Be Spoken Silently

(Based on 'A Poem to be Spoken Silently' by Pie Corbett)

It was so quiet
I could hear my heart pumping
Like a jack hammer.

It was so silent
I could hear an ant's footstep
Like an elephant on Mars.

It was so still
I could hear a jet from miles away
Like an earthquake.

Shaun Johnson (9)
Beck Primary School

A Poem To Be Spoken Silently

(Based on 'A Poem to be Spoken Silently' by Pie Corbett)

It was so quiet
I heard an elephant trumpeting
At the other side of the world.

It was so quiet
I heard a single hair falling
Softly on the marble floor.

It was so quiet
I heard a tiny raindrop floating
Onto the soft green grass.

It was so quiet
I heard a sunflower growing
In the silky grass.

Summer Hawnt (8)
Beck Primary School

Open The Door

Open the door slowly
Hope you don't get poorly
Open the door and peep inside
Hope you don't get a nasty surprise
Weird, weird, just as I feared
Make sure you don't get sheared.

Hannah Walker (8)
Beck Primary School

A Poem To Be Spoken Silently

(Based on 'A Poem to be Spoken Silently' by Pie Corbett)

It was so quiet
That I heard a spider spinning its silky web
As it spins in knots and loops

It was so silent
That I heard a beautiful red sunset
Rising up before me

It was so still
That I heard the massive white clouds
Bouncing up and down in the wind

It was so peaceful
That I heard the see-through ghosts
Whistling as they sway to and fro

It was so still
That I heard the books chatting
As their pages go back and forth

It was so quiet
That I heard a child dreaming
As she kicked her feet

It was so silent
That I heard a black bat talk to the steamed-up window
As a raindrop slid down it

It was so still
I heard a purple flower sing
Until dawn.

Kelsey Hallam (9)
Beck Primary School

A Poem To Be Spoken Silently

(Based on 'A Poem to be Spoken Silently' by Pie Corbett)

It was so quiet
That I heard a hedgehog
Crunch up into a ball.

It was so peaceful
That I heard an eyebrow
Tick and shut.

It was so quiet
That I heard a feather drop.

It was so quiet
That I heard a hamster squealing.

It was so quiet
That I heard a cat peering.

It was so quiet
That I heard a fish jump out of water.

It was so quiet
That I heard a net bounce out of the back.

It was so quiet
That I heard a rat running.

Elliot Flint (8)
Beck Primary School

A Poem To Be Spoken Silently

(Based on 'A Poem to be Spoken Silently' by Pie Corbett)

It was so quiet
That I heard a huge black spider
Quickly creeping over a web
As it rebuilt its home.

It was so peaceful
That I heard a colourful rainbow
Slowly rising in the morning sky.

It was so silent
That I heard the green plants silently growing
While they stood beside the window.

It was so still
That I heard my eyes constantly blinking
As they looked around the room.

It was so calm
That I heard a cute dog with a rabbit's tail
Wishing he could wag it.

Keziah Saunders (8)
Beck Primary School

A Poem To Be Spoken Silently

(Based on 'A Poem to be Spoken Silently' by Pie Corbett)

It was so quiet
That I heard the flower buds pop
As they reached for the sky.

It was so still
That I heard the leaves rustling under my feet
And leaves falling on my head.

It was so calm
That I heard a mouse tap dancing downstairs.

It was so peaceful
That I heard my breath swallowing down my throat.

It was so quiet
That I heard the strawberries and oranges
Dancing downstairs.

Charlotte Smart (9)
Beck Primary School

A Poem To Be Spoken Silently

(Based on 'A Poem to be Spoken Silently' by Pie Corbett)

It was so quiet
That I heard a spider make its web.

It was so peaceful
That I heard a keyboard clicking.

It was so still
That I heard a mouse crawling.

Michael Smith (8)
Beck Primary School

A Poem To Be Spoken Silently

(Based on 'A Poem to be Spoken Silently' by Pie Corbett)

It was so quiet
That I heard the colourful rainbow
Rising in the beautiful blue sky.

It was so quiet
That I heard my beautiful blue eyes
Blinking slowly.

It was so quiet
That I heard the clock ticking
On the wall.

It was so quiet
That I heard a bud opening
Into a beautiful flower.

It was so quiet
That I heard the bright yellow sun
Hiding behind the fluffy clouds.

It was so quiet
That I heard the birds singing
In the breeze.

Blake Wilson (9)
Beck Primary School

A Poem To Be Spoken Silently

(Based on 'A Poem to be Spoken Silently' by Pie Corbett)

It was so quiet
That I heard a mouse
Playing on the keyboard.

It was so silent
That I heard rats
Tap dancing.

It was so calm
That I heard cats singing.

Sherridan Green (9)
Beck Primary School

A Poem To Be Spoken Silently

(Based on 'A Poem to be Spoken Silently' by Pie Corbett)

It was so quiet
That I heard an egg crack in the kitchen.

It was so peaceful
That I heard a slug eating a plant.

It was so still
That I heard writing on white paper.

It was so silent
That I heard a blinking black eye in the Monday morning.

It was so still
That I heard teeth clicking.

It was so calm
I could hear a spider making a web.

Abby Pearce (8)
Beck Primary School

A Poem To Be Spoken Silently

(Based on 'A Poem to be Spoken Silently' by Pie Corbett)

It was so quiet
That I heard my pen
Scraping across the board.

It was so peaceful
That I heard my heartbeat.

It was so silent
That I heard the rats dancing.

Sophie Wilson (9)
Beck Primary School

A Poem To Be Spoken Silently
(Based on 'A Poem to be Spoken Silently' by Pie Corbett)

It was so silent I could hear . . .
The wind whispering, 'Are we there yet?'

It was so tranquil that I could hear . . .
A ladybird's footsteps padding across a hole-ridden leaf.

It was so soundless that I could hear . . .
The Atlantic Ocean swaying and swishing softly.

It was so still that I could hear . . .
The *squeak* of a mouse next door.

It was so quiet that I could hear . . .
The splash of a rainbow a mile away!

Keiran Roome (9)
Beck Primary School

A Poem To Be Spoken Silently
(Based on 'A Poem to be Spoken Silently' by Pie Corbett)

It was so quiet
I heard the pop of a bubble in a fish tank.

It was so silent
I heard the sound of a feather falling out of a pillow.

It was so silent
That I heard my heart beating.

It was so quiet
That I heard my bones walking.

It was so calm
That I heard my boots on the pure white snow.

Emma-Louise Harper (8)
Beck Primary School

A Poem To Be Spoken Silently

(Based on 'A Poem to be Spoken Silently' by Pie Corbett)

It was so quiet that I could hear
A ladybird's footsteps as it walked around my feet.

It was so peaceful that I could hear
My own footsteps as I walked in the golden soft sand.

It was so calm that I could hear
Popcorn crackling in my mouth.

It was so still that I could hear
The noise of owls tweeting their songs.

It was so soundless I could sense
The trees dancing to and fro.

Laura Embley (8)
Beck Primary School

A Poem To Be Spoken Silently

(Based on 'A Poem to be Spoken Silently' by Pie Corbett)

It was so tranquil that I could hear
The sand flying past the window.

It was so peaceful that I could hear
A barbeque cooking sweet fish.

It was so still that I could hear
The board pen write on the whiteboard.

It was so whispery that I could hear
My heart beating.

It was so soundless that I could hear
My bones growing.

It was so quiet that I could hear
The sun's rays sing.

It was so calm that I could hear
My boots walking along the white snow.

Nicole Kennedy (8)
Beck Primary School

A Poem To Be Spoken Silently
(Based on 'A Poem to be Spoken Silently' by Pie Corbett)

It was so tranquil I could hear
The sound of a caterpillar growing wings in a cocoon.

It was so soundless that I could hear
The sound of a sponge in a bath.

It was so peaceful that I could hear
The sound of a ladybird's footsteps stepping on a leaf.

It was so calm that I could hear
The sound of a giant piece of rock wishing not to be there.

It was so still that I could hear
The sound of a tear running down someone's face, crying.

David Burnham (9)
Beck Primary School

A Poem To Be Spoken Silently
(Based on 'A Poem to be Spoken Silently' by Pie Corbett)

It was so quiet I could hear
The footsteps of a ladybird.

It was so peaceful I could hear
The blinking of my eyelashes!

It was so calm that I could hear
The crackling of the popcorn!

It was so still that I could hear
A monkey swinging from tree to tree.

It was so noiseless I could hear
A mouse creep on the floor!

Tiffany Rebecca Gibbs (9)
Beck Primary School

A Poem To Be Spoken Silently

(Based on 'A Poem to be Spoken Silently' by Pie Corbett)

It was so quiet I heard
A ladybird's footsteps on a leaf.

It was so tranquil that I could hear
Ants collecting leaves.

It was so peaceful that I could hear
Hedgehogs shuffling across the road.

It was so noiseless that I could hear
Squirrels chomping on nuts.

It was so calm I could hear
The ocean swaying from side to side.

Ellie Victoria Lister (8)
Beck Primary School

A Poem To Be Spoken Silently

(Based on 'A Poem to be Spoken Silently' by Pie Corbett)

It was so quiet
That I could hear a mouse.

It was so peaceful
That I could hear a footstep.

It was so still
That I could hear a wolf.

It was so calm
That I could sense the fish swimming in the sea.

Katlin Kilner (8)
Beck Primary School

A Poem To Be Spoken Silently

(Based on 'A Poem to be Spoken Silently' by Pie Corbett)

It was so quiet that I heard
The whispering of the raindrops falling.

It was so peaceful that I heard
A pin drop down from the table.

It was so still that I heard
A frog bouncing on a lily pad.

It was so silent that I heard
The ladybird walking on the leaf.

It was so calm that I heard
The book page turn over in the library.

It was so still that I heard
The snow coming down from the sky.

It was so quiet that I heard
The grass growing.

Zoe Slingsby (8)
Beck Primary School

Opening The Door

Opening the door
Easy, easy
Open the door
Making sure it is slow
Make it delicate
And divine
Making sure
You close it behind.

Chantelle Wright (7)
Beck Primary School

Weather

I like summer because it is
Nice and hot
But I will get a lot of spots
Winter is the season
That gets very cold
If I don't wear a hat
I could become bald
When it is warm
You can play in the pool
It's a lot better
Than being in school
But at Christmas time
It's very snowy
In the summer the trees
Are lovely and green
When the winter is white
I may get frostbite
But I will go on my sleigh
And go out to play.

Bethany Jones (10)
Beck Primary School

Snowing

Frost settles on the path,
As dawn comes,
People scurry out of houses,
Into the icy wind.

Isabel Edain (7)
Beck Primary School

Celebrations

A very merry wine and sherry Christmas,
Lots of presents for you and me,
Living under the Christmas tree.
Christmas weather is sometimes murky,
People always eat a turkey.
I wish this tradition hadn't come,
Poor little turkey, run, run, *run!*
Run before the farmer gets you,
Run before he sells or bets you,
He'll kill you quickly, short and sweet,
Then he'll sell your bodily meat.
Every year it's the same,
Oh, I wish this tradition never came.
At least there is a happy new year,
Filled with fun and packed with cheer.
A new year is a new start,
But the food from Christmas could make you part.
At Easter we have lots of chocolate eggs,
Then we work the fat off our legs.
Bonfire Night is really great,
It's the people that I really hate.
The people who blow up things with noisy rockets,
People who stuff fireworks in their pockets.
There are always casualties on Bonfire Night,
See the blood pour, what a sight!
On birthdays there's a special treat . . .
. . . a delicious birthday cake to eat!

Joseph Wall (10)
Beck Primary School

Love

L oving someone warms the heart
O ver if been made a fool
V ery many people are in love
E verlasting love.

Kay Hartley (10)
Beck Primary School

Winter

W indy, strong wind blowing off colourful leaves from the branches
 I ce too slippery and smooth, shining in the morning sun
N o going out to call for your friends, for outdoor fun
 T oes of families toasting in front of the fire, keeping safe and warm
E nvelopes of Christmas cards spreading Christmas cheer
R oasting yummy chicken in the oven for you to enjoy.

Kerri Walker (9)
Beck Primary School

A Poem To Be Spoken Silently

(Based on 'A Poem to be Spoken Silently' by Pie Corbett)

It was so quiet that I heard
The trees blown by the wind.

It was so peaceful that I heard
The leaves falling off the trees.

It was so silent that I heard
Flowers whispering to each other.

It was so still that I heard
My friend calling me.

It was so calm that I heard
The ground shaking.

It was so silent that I heard
A stranger coming in.

Natasha Sigauke (8)
Beck Primary School

The Viking Longship Kennings

Dragon-header
Wave-traveller
Ocean-surfer
Sea-warrior
Soul-scarer.

Joseph Burley (9)
Beck Primary School

An Autumn Leaf

Watch me soar through the air, I am soaring,
Soaring like a bird in the sky.
Watch me twirl through the air, I am twirling,
Twirling like a dancer way up high.

Watch me dance through the air, I am dancing,
Dancing with the wind, I am free.
Watch me glide through the air, I am gliding,
Gliding with the clouds, to the sea.

Watch me spin through the air, I am spinning,
Spinning down to the ground, round and round.
Watch me stay in a pile, I will stay there,
Stay there till I crumble to the ground.

But hope is not lost,
As the ground will call,
I will feed another tree
And another leaf will fall.

Neena Dugar (9)
Hill House St Mary's School

Nature's Offers

Nature offers me . . . the wind and rain and sea
Wind is like beating drums against my window.
Howling loudly, freezing me with fright
Making noises like werewolves growling.

Rain drizzles down from the dreary, gloomy sky
Like fine tears, spitting down its emotions.
Rain dancing and bouncing off the ground
Making music like an orchestra of tambourines.

Waves of the sea rise like an angry sea monster
With white foam dribbling from the mouth
Of the navy-blue sea creature.
Water shining in the sunlight, looks like someone
Has sprinkled glitter all over the sea.

Nature offers me . . . stars glistening in the pitch-black darkness
Lighting the way like a thousand glittering torches.
The fiery comets blasting and zooming, leaving a trail of orange
Yellow and red flashes like sparklers on Bonfire Night.
The swirly white Milky Way looks like the cream in my Swiss roll
Being delicious in the darkness!

Nature offers me . . . leaves from a tree
I love to throw leaves and smother others in the breeze.
Jubilant faces glow like light bulbs, as we play in the leaves
We love to pile them into mounds of burnt, blurred colours
And swing our legs back and forth and then, start again.

That is what nature offers me . . . and it's all for free!

Safia Khan (8)
Hill House St Mary's School

Sunsets In Hawaii

The sky is pink as the night is nigh,
The sun drifting away.

Singing their last songs for the day,
High in the monkey puzzle trees birds finish.

The crickets click repertoires,
As the sun gradually dances into the night.

Amber clouds glisten as they float
With sparkling stars shining through them.

Tides come in washing noble sand sculptures away,
With a pinky blue sea sucking it in and spitting it out.

Beach shops closing, street lights turning on
And young children going to bed.

Colours decorating the sky
Not pink, nor gold, neither amber, but somehow . . .
All three splashed about the sky.

Out of all the countries Hawaii's sunsets are the best
They have inspiration and art
That's the sunsets in Hawaii.

Amelia Laura Nettleton (8)
Hill House St Mary's School

Football

Football is a great game,
If you win, you get fame,
Training on a morning,
Makes me all a-yawning.

Running round keeps you fit,
Just take care not to slip,
All lined up for a goal,
One big kick, in it goes.

What a team, what a score,
Can you hear the crowd roar,
Man of the match, I am
I'm Zinedine Zidane.

Here we are, with the cup,
What a game, what good luck,
We go home, with a smile,
Football really is worthwhile!

Joshua Clarke (10)
Hill House St Mary's School

Body

Smile, frown, laugh and cry,
They are all the same.
Jump, step, hop and limp,
They are all the same.

We are one,
They are one
And put together we can be great.

So use your brains
And think, what could it mean?
What is one?
It's your body!

Rowena Eves (9)
Hill House St Mary's School

My Guitar

When the famous rock star flicks my strings
The sound is amazing
I can be electric or acoustic
When I'm played on the stage
I feel like the best guitar ever
I get played solo and accompanied
The brand new strings are pulled
To make clear, crisp sounds
That always get the crowd roaring
My metallic frets change the pitch
Making the notes get higher and higher
I can play longer and louder notes when I'm electric
And short and quiet notes when I'm acoustic
My dazzling body, which is as yellow as the sun
Shines brightly in the stage lights
The plain silver machine heads tune my strings
To make the sound just right
My sounds are *strum, strum, pluck, pluck*
Twang, twang, ping, ping . . .

Thomas Hale (9)
Holy Rood RC Primary School

The Smooth Snake

The snake weaves gracefully
The snake slithers down the tree
The snake has a beady eye
The snake spied on the mouse
The snake has long fangs full of poison
The snake spied a fat bird, put it down
And went to sleep.

Polly Clark (10)
Holy Rood RC Primary School

Loud Lucy

Loud Lucy is her name
Shouting is her game
She shouts and bawls
Rants and raves
All the attention she always craves.

She bangs and rattles
Like a Tommy gun
She needs a staple
Putting through her tongue.

But one day Lucy has to learn
That shouting and bawling her voice will pay
She'll wake up one morning and not a sound will make
But for the rest of us, peace, it will break.

Anna McNicholas (9)
Holy Rood RC Primary School

The Cat And Mouse

The cat waiting
The mouse staring
The cat pouncing
The mouse staring
The cat landing
The mouse running
The cat running
The mouse stopping
The cat pouncing
The mouse staring
The cat landing
The mouse dying
The cat leaving
The mouse bleeding
The cat miaowing.

Mollie Prentice (10)
Holy Rood RC Primary School

Doctor Who

The TARDIS whirling round and round
Dr Who has come to ground
People look up to the sky
Alien spaceships are flashing by
Daleks, Cybermen, fought them all
One by one, they always fall
Rose and the Doctor our only hope
Without them, how would we cope?
Battlestations, battlestations, enemy is near
The Doctor and Rose know no fear.

Amy Bell (10)
Holy Rood RC Primary School

Season

S is for summer when the sun is hot
E is for Easter where the bunny hops high
A is for August when the red rustling leaves blow about
S is for gleaming snow which flows in winter
O is for October when the cold wind blows
N is for new trees which will bloom in summer.

Lydia Athey (9)
Rudston Preparatory School

My Idol

Idols, idols who will it be?
Idols, idols maybe my dad or maybe me.
Idols, idols who could it be?
Idols, idols my dad, definitely!

Oliver Bingham (8)
Rudston Preparatory School

Ronaldo The Great

Cristiano Ronaldo, his flicks and tricks equal a great shot
That flows through the air, then gets at the back of the net
People say he cheats, I don't believe it
The Man United scorer will glory in every game
They boo him, laugh at him, but I don't care
He's the greatest player for Man U, that's never a doubt
His skills thrill me in every game that I watch
It looks like the ball is attracted to him and never leaves him.

Jordan Falding (9)
Rudston Preparatory School

Santa Claus

Santa Claus is coming to town
When the clock strikes midnight
He will be here from the North Pole
To deliver all the presents to the children
That have been good
Then he will go back to the North Pole
For another year, Christmas in 2007.

Umar Farouk (8)
Rudston Preparatory School

Rudston School Poem

S uper, snappy school
C ool, clever school
H appy, healthy school
O rdinary, obedient school
O rganised, old school
L ovely, large school.

Molly Blackburn (8)
Rudston Preparatory School

Flowers

Roses and tulips, lavender too
Pansies and daffodils, they are for you
Flowers, flowers, colourful and bright
They will bloom, morning and night.

Daisies, forget-me-nots, poppies and co
I love all flowers, did you know?
Flowers, flowers, colourful and bright
They will bloom, morning and night.

Alicia Harrison (8)
Rudston Preparatory School

Families

F amilies spend lots of time together
A unties are your cousins Mum
M um and Dad are your closest people
I won't want my mum and dad to split up
L ove is what you need from your family
Y ou are most important to your mum and dad!

Claudia Longdon (9)
Rudston Preparatory School

Dreaming

D ream in vanilla milk
R ed poppies everywhere
E verlasting cookies are very yummy
A pples made out of toffee in my tummy
M ilky Bars I love to eat are stunning
I ce pops, lots of colours, like the rainbow
N etball, my favourite game
G orgeous things are everywhere.

Umara Malik (8)
Rudston Preparatory School

Winter

Winter is cold and snowy
Winter is the time to wrap up warm
Winter is when you build snowmen and have a snowball fight
Winter is when Santa comes and brings you presents
Winter is white, winter is the time to go skiing
In winter there is holly and mince pie wrappers blowing in the wind
Winter is the best time of the year.

Emily Miles (9)
Rudston Preparatory School

New Day

Snuggle into bed,
Turn out the lights,
Get ready for a new day.
Think of all the good things
Just waiting there to be done.
Think of the food, the TV, the computer
And most of all, the care.
Dream and dream and dream
Of things that are wonderful.
Think of all the good things
And think of a good day,
A new day.

Amelia Qaiyum (8)
Rudston Preparatory School

Rain

R is for run or you will get soaked
A is for air, cut through like a knife
I is for incredible, rain runs like a horse
N is for nice with an autumn breeze

Rain is as wet as a dog's nose
Comes with thunder and lightning.

Madhav Padmakumar (9)
Rudston Preparatory School

All About Family

F amily are people who care about you
A unties are people who visit you
M ums and dads are people who look after you
I want my family to be happy
L is for love, which you have all the time
Y is for your youngest sister or brother who you play with.

Olivia Tong (9)
Rudston Preparatory School

The Fiery Dragon

Once, there lived a great big blue *dragon!*
Its ivory, dagger-like spikes on its back,
Its knife-long teeth, shaped like an axe,
It lived in a large cave,
Somewhere in Wales,
Nobody knew about him,
Fiery dragon.

Mohammad Hammad Hasain Raza (8)
Rudston Preparatory School

Circuits

C is for circuit which we build
I is for insulator like plastic
R is for rubber insulating the electricity
C is for conductor, electricity flowing through
U is for understanding, most people do
I is for including the other equipment
T is for testing the material
S is for science, that I like to do!

Alice Swann (9)
Rudston Preparatory School

Christmas Day

C hristmas is brilliant
H ow do you get to sleep?
R *attle, rattle*, I spring from my bed
I think, *is he here?*
S anta, Santa, he must be here
T *ap, tap*, I hope he has drunk his beer
'M arion, Marion,' I tiptoe into her room,
'A re you coming?' 'Of course I am.'
'S anta has been . . . Mum! Santa has been . . . Dad'

D ad is still in bed
A ll we can hear is a noisy snore
Y ippee, it's Christmas!

Lawrence Hancock (9)
Rudston Preparatory School

Battery

B atteries use chemical energy
A is for attaching a battery to wires
T is for thinking hard to make a circuit
T is for taking care of yourself
E lectricity passing through the battery
R is for reading instructions on the battery
Y is for you plugging a battery into a battery holder.

Dominic Walsham (8)
Rudston Preparatory School

Summer

S un is hot, burning bright
U nder a tree is cool and dark
M um is sunbathing
M um gets burnt
E dward gets wet
R upert plays ball.

Nicole Vasey (9)
Rudston Preparatory School

Chocolate

C hocolate is sweet
H ot chocolate is yummy
O pen that cupboard
C hocolate is heaven
O range flavour is what I like
L ittle Celebrations dance around
A ngels melt into chocolate
T en chocolates for me
E xciting chocolate.

Paige Gibbons (8)
Rudston Preparatory School

Who Killed The Hen?

(Based on 'Who Killed Cock Robin?' by Anon)

Who's killed the hen?
'I,' remarked the ox,
'With my best buddy, the fox,
I killed the hen.'

Who saw them drop?
'I,' commented the pig,
'As I started to dig,
I saw them drop.'

Who'll catch their blood?
'I,' explained the fish,
'With my red dish,
I'll catch the blood.'

Who'll make the shroud?
'I,' announced the lizard,
'With my friend, Blizzard,
I'll make the shroud.'

Who'll dig the grave?
'I,' mentioned the storm,
'As I completed the form,
I'll dig their grave.'

Sandy Ireland (10)
Sandringham Primary School

Who Killed The Iguanodon?

(Based on 'Who Killed Cock Robin?' by Anon)

Who killed the iguanodon?
'I,' said the allosaurus,
'With my thick and deadly thesaurus,
I killed the iguanodon.'

Who saw her death?
'I,' said the diplodocus,
'With my very strong focus,
I saw her death.'

Who caught her blood?
'I,' said the brachiosaurus,
'With my extremely fat walrus,
I caught her blood.'

Who'll make the shroud?
'I,' said T-rex, 'with my very useful text,
I'll make the shroud.'

Who'll dig the grave?
'I,' said the stegosaurus,
'In this universe,
I'll dig her grave.'

Who'll carry the coffin?
'I,' said the triceratops,
'Wearing multicolour tops,
I'll carry the coffin.'

Who'll sing a prayer?
'I,' said the velociraptor,
'With my tractor,
I'll sing a prayer.'

Who'll bury her?
'I,' said jontasaurus,
'With help from diplodocus,
I'll bury her.'

Who'll watch her be buried?
'I,' said the silophisus,
'In this crisis,
I'll watch her be buried.'

Shannon Hughes (11)
Sandringham Primary School

Who Killed The Daddy-Long-Legs?

(Based on 'Who Killed Cock Robin?' by Anon)

Who killed the daddy-long-legs?
'I,' said the praying mantis,
'I killed him with my deadly kiss,
I killed the daddy-long-legs.'

Who saw him die?
'I,' said the millipede,
'While I was planting my massive seeds,
I saw him die?'

Who'll make the shroud?
'I,' said the spider,
'While I'm drinking my exceedingly sweet cider,
I'll make the shroud.'

Who caught the blood?
'I,' said the snail,
'While I was talking to my fantastic friend, the whale,
I caught his blood.'

Who'll dig the grave?
'I,' said the worm,
'With my excellent spade that's firm,
I'll dig the grave.'

Who'll carry the coffin?
'I,' said the ladybird,
'I'll carry it while I'm doing my crossword,
I'll carry the coffin.'

Who'll be the chief mourner?
'I,' said the slug,
'Even though I always hated that bug,
I'll be the chief mourner.'

Who'll sing the psalm?
'I,' said the grasshopper,
'With my very large chopper,
I'll sing the psalm.'

Who'll say the prayer?
'I,' said the caterpillar,
'With my real shining star,
I'll say the prayer.'

Some of the bugs stared in sorrow,
While the others started to follow.

Kelly Howe (10)
Sandringham Primary School

Who Killed The Daddy-Long-Legs?

(Based on 'Who Killed Cock Robin' by Anon)

Who killed the daddy-long-legs?
'I,' said the praying mantis,
'I hit him so hard, I hit him with my bucket of lard,
I killed the daddy-long-legs.'

Who saw him die?
'I,' said the millipede,
While I was putting in a hair bead,
I saw him die.'

Who'll make the shroud?
'I,' said the spider,
'I'll make it so it's as nifty as a glider,
I'll made the shroud.'

Who'll carry the coffin?
'I,' said the ladybird,
'I'll make it so there's not a word,
I'll carry the coffin.'

Who'll dig the grave?
'I,' said the snail,
'With my shovel and my pail,
I'll dig the grave.'

Who'll be chief mourner?
'I,' said the ant,
'While I'm watering my plant,
I'll be chief mourner.'

Who'll sing the psalm?
'I,' said the grasshopper,
'With the help of my friend, the copper,
I'll sing the psalm.'

Who'll toll the bell?
'I,' said the caterpillar,
'Because I'm right next to it, stuck in tar,
I'll toll the bell.'

All the bugs bowed their heads
As poor daddy-long-legs
He was dead.

George Gears (10)
Sandringham Primary School

Who Killed The Ladybird?

(Based on 'Who Killed Cock Robin?' by Anon)

Who killed the ladybird?
'I,' said the spider,
'With the strength of a tiger,
I killed the ladybird.'

Who saw her die?
'I,' said the ant,
'From behind the plant,
I saw her die.'

Who will make the shroud?
'I,' said the bee,
'It's easy for me,
I will make the shroud.'

Who will dig the grave?
'I,' said the earwig,
'With a jig,
I will dig the grave.'

Who will be the vicar?
'I,' said the slug,
'With my holy rug,
I'll be the vicar.'

Who will carry the coffin?
'I,' said the dragonfly,
'I can fly high,
I'll carry the coffin.'

Who will be the chief mourner?
'I,' said the woodlice,
'Rolling my dice,
I'll be the chief mourner.'

Who will sing the song?
'I,' said the mosquito,
'I sing with an echo,
I'll sing the song.'

Who will toll the bell?
'I,' said the caterpillar,
'I'm strong, like a builder,
I'll toll the bell.'

Dominic Farrow (10)
Sandringham Primary School

Who's Killed The Dog?

(Based on 'Who Killed Cock Robin?' by Anon)

Who's killed the dog?
'I,' remarked the frog,
'With my big log,
I've killed the dog.'

Who saw him drop?
'I,' peered the cat,
'And I was wearing a hat,
I saw him drop.'

Who'll catch his blood?
'I,' announced the fish,
'With my little blue dish,
I'll catch the blood.'

Who'll make the shroud?
'I,' replied the bat,
'With the help from a rat,
I'll make the shroud.'

Who'll dig the grave?
'I,' slithered the snake,
'With the help of my rake,
I'll dig the grave.'

Grant Littledyke (11)
Sandringham Primary School

Who Killed The Daddy-Long-Legs?

(Based on 'Who Killed Cock Robin?' by Anon)

Who killed the daddy-long-legs?
'I,' said the praying mantis,
'I killed him with my deadly kiss,
I killed the daddy-long-legs.'

Who saw him die?
'I,' said the millipede,
'I also saw him bleed,
I saw him die.'

Who'll make a shroud?
'I,' said the spider,
'While I drink my nice, but strong, cider,
I'll make the shroud.'

Who'll catch the blood?
'I,' said the snail,
'While I'm talking to my mate, the whale,
I'll catch the blood.'

Who'll dig the grave?
'I,' said the worm,
'With my shovel that's firm,
I'll dig the grave.'

Who'll carry the coffin?
'I,' said the ladybird,
'The silence will not be stirred,
I'll carry the coffin.'

Who'll be the chief mourner?
'I,' said the slimy slug,
'I'll say my last goodbye to that bug,
I'll be the chief mourner.'

Who'll sing the song?
'I,' said the grasshopper,
'With my very large chopper,
I'll sing the song.'

Who'll say the prayer?
'I,' said the caterpillar,
'While I'm holding my fluffy pillow,
I'll say the prayer.'

All the bugs
Fell down in sorrow
As for the daddy-long-legs
There is no tomorrow.

Jessica Beardmore (11)
Sandringham Primary School

Who Killed The Rabbit?

(Based on 'Who Killed Cock Robin?' by Anon)

Who's killed the rabbit?
'I,' said the beetle,
'I injected the rabbit with my big needle,
I've killed the rabbit.'

Who sees them drop?
'I,' responded the lizard,
'As I was camouflaged in the blizzard,
I see them drop.'

Who'll catch the blood?
'I,' explained the lion,
'As I was hunting my pray with my iron,
I'll catch the blood.'

Who'll make the shroud?
'I,' answered the rat,
'I will make it with my flying mat,
I'll make the shroud.'

Who'll dig the grave?
'I,' whispered the stork,
'As I am digging the grave with my big cork,
I'll dig the grave.'

John Austin (10)
Sandringham Primary School

Who Killed Kitty Cat?

(Based on 'Who Killed Cock Robin?' by Anon)

Who killed kitty cat?
'I,' stammered the dog,
'With my warty frog,
I killed kitty cat.'

Who saw her die?
'I,' mentioned the fly,
'While I was telling a lie,
I saw her die.'

Who caught her blood?
'I,' sighed the parrot,
'With my whole carrot,
I caught her blood.'

Who'll make the shroud?
'I,' exclaimed the rabbit,
'I do it for a habit,
I'll make the shroud.'

Who'll dig her grave?
'I,' croaked the frog,
'With my sharp log,
I'll dig her grave.'

Who'll be the parson?
'I,' said the duck,
'With my little book,
I'll be the parson.'

Who'll be the clerk?
'We will,' screeched the ants,
'In our pink pants,
We'll be the clerk.'

Who'll carry the link?
'I,' replied the mole,
'With my bowl,
I'll carry the link.'

Who'll be chief mourner?
'I,' suggested fur,
'I'll give a little purr,
I'll be the chief mourner.'

Who'll carry her coffin?
'I,' squeaked the mouse,
'With my little louse,
I'll carry her coffin.'

Who'll bear the pall?
'We will,' squealed the hens,
'While we're sitting in our pens,
We'll bear the pall.'

Who'll sing the psalm?
'I,' snapped the crocodile,
'While I'm swimming down the Nile,
I'll sing the psalm.'

Georgia Dikaioylia (11)
Sandringham Primary School

Who Killed The Gerbil?

(Based on 'Who Killed Cock Robin?' by Anon)

Who killed the gerbil?
'I,' announced the cat,
'With my baseball bat,
I killed the gerbil.'

Who saw him die?
'I,' mumbled the bee,
'Because I can see,
I saw him die.'

Who caught his blood?
'I,' mentioned the spider,
'With my can of cider,
I caught his blood.'

Who'll make the shroud?
'I,' exclaimed the sparrow,
'With my little arrow,
I'll make the shroud.'

Who'll dig his grave?
'I,' suggested the guinea pig,
'Because I can dig,
I'll dig his grave.'

Who'll be the parson?
'I,' stuttered the parrot,
'With my carrot,
I'll be the parson.'

Who'll be the clerk?
'I,' sneered the rabbit,
'I'll make it a habit,
I'll be the clerk.'

Who'll carry the link?
'I,' snapped the dog,
'I'll practise on my log,
I'll carry the link.'

Who'll be the chief mourner?
'I,' snarled the lizard,
'If it's not in a blizzard,
I'll be the chief mourner.'

Who'll carry the coffin?
'I,' answered the moth,
'When I get rid of this cough,
I'll carry the coffin.'

Who'll bear the pall?
'We,' murmured the mice,
'What about our rice?
We'll bear the pall.'

Who'll sing the psalm?
'I,' cried the fly,
'I'll try not to cry,
I'll sing the psalm.'

Who'll toll the bell?
'I,' replied the rain,
'With my swinging cane,
I'll toll the bell.'

Jake Grantham (11)
Sandringham Primary School

Who Killed The Hawk?

(Based on 'Who Killed Cock Robin?' by Anon)

Who killed the hawk?
'I,' remarked the eagle,
'With my buddy, the seagull,
We killed the hawk.'

Who saw him die?
'I,' commented the monkey,
'Because I'm very hunky,
I saw him die.'

Who caught his blood?
'I,' responded the lizard,
'With my blizzard,
I caught his blood.'

Who'll make the shroud?
'I,' replied the spider,
'As I start to drink my cider,
I'll make the shroud.'

Who'll dig the grave?
'I,' announced the pig,
'I'll start to dig,
I'll dig his grave.'

Who'll be the parson?
'I,' said the rook,
'With this book,
I'll be the parson.'

Who'll be the clerk?
'I,' uttered the cloud,
'As I'm very proud,
I'll be the clerk.'

Who'll carry the link?
'I,' retorted the linnet,
'I'll fetch it in a minute,
I'll carry the link.'

Who'll be chief mourner?
'I,' remarked the dove,
'I'll mourn for my love,
I'll be chief mourner.'

Who'll carry the coffin?
'I,' mentioned the lark,
'As long as it's not dark,
I'll carry the coffin.'

Who'll bear the pall?
'I,' declared the hare,
'As long as I don't get a scare,
I'll bear the pall.'

Who'll sing the psalm?
'I,' exclaimed the robin,
'I'll sing by sobbing,
I'll sing the psalm.'

Who'll toll the bell?
'I,' stated the golden eagle,
'Standing proud and regal,
I'll toll the bell.'

Jordan Perkins (10)
Sandringham Primary School

Who Killed Reed The Rabbit?

(Based on 'Who Killed Cock Robin?' by Anon)

Who killed Reed the rabbit?
'I,' sighed the scarecrow,
'With this big bow,
I killed Reed the rabbit.'

Who saw him die?
'I,' explained the mole,
'In my little hole,
I saw him die.'

Who caught his blood?
'I,' cried the mouse,
'In my tree house,
I caught his blood.'

Who'll make the shroud?
'I,' mentioned the daisy,
'Even though I'm lazy,
I'll make the shroud.'

Who'll dig his grave?
'I,' replied the spider,
'With my blue glider,
I'll dig his grave.'

Who'll be the parson?
'I,' jeered the snake,
'But first I have to bake,
I'll be the parson.'

Who'll sing the psalm?
'I,' replied the goose,
'When I've eaten this chocolate mousse,
I'll sing the psalm.'

Who'll carry the link?
'I,' scoffed the mud,
'Even though I'm a dud,
I'll carry the link.'

Who'll be the chief mourner?
'I,' laughed the leaf,
'When I've eaten my beef,
I'll be the chief mourner.'

Who'll carry the coffin?
'I,' hinted the lake,
'When I wake,
I'll carry the coffin.'

Who'll bear the pall?
'I,' commented the tree,
'When I catch a bee,
I'll bear the pall.'

Who'll toll the bell?
'I,' responded the crow,
'When I eat some dough,
I'll toll the bell.'

Joshua Wilburn (10)
Sandringham Primary School

Who Killed The Dog?

(Based on 'Who Killed Cock Robin?' by Anon)

Who killed the dog?
'I,' responded the cattle,
'We had a ferocious battle,
I killed the dog.'

Who saw him die?
'I,' declared the seed,
'With my little weed,
I saw him die.'

Who caught his blood?
'I,' answered the nettle,
'Just as it started to settle,
I caught his blood.'

Who'll make the shroud?
'I,' cried the bear,
'With my little hare,
I'll make the shroud.'

Who'll dig the grave?
'I,' snarled the breeze,
'With a little help from the trees,
I'll dig the grave.'

Who'll be the parson?
'I,' jeered Bella,
As she was drinking Stella,
'I'll be the parson.'

Who'll be the clerk?
'I,' muttered Honey,
As the day was sunny,
'I'll be the clerk.'

Who'll carry the link?
'I,' remarked the thunder,
As everyone began to wonder,
'I'll carry the link.'

Who'll be chief mourner?
'I,' sneered the willow,
As it dozed on a pillow,
'I'll be chief mourner.'

Who'll carry the coffin?
'I,' stuttered the snake,
'I'm not fake,
I'll carry the coffin.'

Who'll bear the pall?
'We will,' whispered the fishes,
As they jumped out of the dishes,
'We'll bear the pall.'

Who'll sing the psalm?
'I,' scoffed the book,
As it was stuck on a hook,
'I'll sing the psalm.'

Who'll toll the bell?
'We will,' stammered the herd,
As all you could hear was the bird,
'We'll toll the bell.'

Laura Hooper (10)
Sandringham Primary School

Who Killed The Dog?

(Based on 'Who Killed Cock Robin?' by Anon)

Who killed the dog?
'I,' miaowed the cat,
Who was as blind as a bat
'I killed the dog.'

Who saw him drop?
'I,' shouted the breeze,
Swaying in the trees,
'I saw him drop.'

Who caught his blood?
'I,' remarked the flea,
Who was jumping with glee,
'I caught his blood.'

Who'll make the shroud?
'I,' sighed the pup,
Who was drinking out of his cup,
'I'll make the shroud.'

Who'll dig the grave?
'I,' yelled the robin,
Who was sat in a tree, sobbing,
'I'll dig the grave.'

Who'll be the parson?
'I,' announced the pig,
Who started to dig,
'I'll be the parson.'

Who'll be the chief mourner?
'I,' cried the plant,
With his pet ant,
'I'll be the chief mourner.'

Who'll carry the coffin?
'I,' snapped the rain,
Who was in terrible pain,
'I'll carry the coffin.'

Who'll sing the psalm?
'I,' shrieked the cloud,
Who was singing so loud,
'I'll sing the psalm.'

Who'll bear the pall?
'I,' sneered the storm,
Who was mowing the lawn,
'I'll bear the pall.'

Who'll toll the bell?
'I,' murmured the mouse,
Who was sat in his little house,
'I'll toll the bell.'

Who'll be the clerk?
'I,' exclaimed the wolf,
As the wolf was playing golf,
'I will be the clerk.'

Leah Sayles (11)
Sandringham Primary School

Who Killed The Rabbit?

(Based on 'Who Killed Cock Robin?' by Anon)

Who killed the rabbit?
'I,' sighed the parrot,
'I shot him with a carrot,
I killed the rabbit.'

Who saw him die?
'I,' remarked the thunder,
'I made him stand back and wonder,
I saw him die.'

Who caught his blood?
'I,' shouted the sun,
'I caught his blood, while I was having fun,
I caught his blood.'

Who'll make the shroud?
'I,' suggested the seed,
'I will knit it with my beads,
I'll make the shroud.'

Who'll dig his grave?
'I,' responded the breeze,
'After I have had my cheese,
I'll dig his grave.'

Who'll be the parson?
'I,' announced the hare,
'While eating a pear,
I'll be the parson.'

Who'll be the clerk?
'I,' replied the cloud so grey,
'I'll do it in the month of May,
I'll be the clerk.'

Who'll carry the link?
'I,' whispered the rain,
As he spoke in pain,
'I'll carry the link.'

Who'll be the chief mourner?
'I,' snapped the sun so bright,
'With all my might,
I'll be the chief mourner.'

Who'll carry the coffin?
'I,' laughed the soil,
He thought he might boil,
'I'll carry the coffin.'

Who'll sing the psalm?
'I,' commented the grass,
'While I pass,
I'll sing the psalm.'

Who'll bear the pall?
'I,' buzzed the bee,
As he flew past the tree,
'I'll bear the pall.'

Who'll toll the bell?
'I,' yelled the cloud,
'I'll be so proud,
I'll toll the bell.'

Maryam Bi (10)
Sandringham Primary School

Who Killed The Whale?

(Based on 'Who Killed Cock Robin?' by Anon)

Who killed the whale?
'I,' mentioned the jellyfish,
'I thought he was a jolly dish,
I killed the whale.'

Who saw him die?
'I,' murmured the moss,
'With my boss,
I saw him die.'

Who caught his blood?
'I,' remarked the sand,
'It landed on my hand,
I caught the blood.'

Who'll make the shroud?
'I,' cried the water,
'Because it was previously knitted by my daughter,
I'll make the shroud.'

Who'll dig the grave?
'I,' snapped the crab,
While eating a kebab,
'I'll dig the grave.'

Who'll be the parson?
'I,' announced the algae,
Looking a bit dowdy,
'I'll be the parson.'

Who'll be the clerk?
'I,' yelled the shark,
'But I can't see in the dark,
I'll be the clerk.'

Who'll carry the link?
'We will,' sneered the stones,
'We'll just put down our bones,
We'll carry the link.'

Who'll be chief mourner?
'I,' growled the seaweed,
    'I'll take the lead,
I'll be the chief mourner.'

Who'll carry the coffin?
'I,' snarled the squid,
As he hid behind a twig,
    'I'll carry the coffin.'

Who'll bear the pall?
'I,' hinted the fish,
As he sat on his dish,
    'I'll bear the pall.'

Who'll sing the psalm?
'I,' stuttered the stingray,
    'But I usually pray,
    I'll sing the psalm.'

Who'll toll the bell?
'I,' stammered the coral,
Whose dress was floral,
    'I'll toll the bell.'

Max Webster (11)
Sandringham Primary School

Who Killed The Gerbil?

(Based on 'Who Killed Cock Robin?' by Anon)

Who killed the gerbil?
'I,' announced the hamster,
Cos I'm a professional gangster,
I killed the gerbil.'

Who saw him die?
'I,' answered the lizard,
'It happened in a terrible blizzard,
I saw him die.'

Who caught his blood?
'I,' declared the fish,
'I caught it with my golden dish,
I caught his blood.'

Who'll make the shroud?
'I,' exclaimed the cat,
'I will dress him in my lucky hat,
I will make the shroud.'

Who'll dig his grave?
'I,' explained the snake,
'I know a perfect place, just by the lake,
I'll dig his grave.'

Who'll be the parson?
'I,' replied the rabbit,
'Reading is my special habit,
I'll be the parson.'

Who'll be the clerk?
'I,' responded the mouse,
'I will do some work at the house,
I'll be the clerk.'

Who'll carry the link?
'I,' responded the tarantula,
'With a little help my from spatula,
I'll carry the link.'

Who'll be the chief mourner?
'I,' suggested the budgie,
'Even though my voice has gone a bit smudgy,
I'll be the chief mourner.'

Who'll carry the coffin?
'I,' shouted the dog,
'I will even make it out of a log,
I'll carry the coffin.'

Who'll bear the pall?
'I,' cried the spider,
'I'll do it while drinking my cider,
I'll bear the pall.'

Who'll sing the psalm?
'I,' yelled the rat,
'But the notes will be flat,
I'll sing the psalm.'

Who'll toll the bell?
'I,' screamed the parrot,
'I will hit it with my juicy carrot,
I'll toll the bell.'

Rebecca Quinn (11)
Sandringham Primary School

Who Killed The Cow?

(Based on 'Who Killed Cock Robin?' by Anon)

Who killed the cow?
'I,' sighed the moon,
'I ate him with a spoon,
I killed the cow.'

Who saw him die?
'I,' explained the dog,
'I was playing with my log,
I saw him die.'

Who caught his blood?
'I,' replied the spider,
'It dropped in my cider,
I caught his blood.'

Who'll make the shroud?
'I,' replied the cat,
'I'll make it with my mat,
I'll make the shroud.'

Who'll dig the grave?
'I,' responded the cloud,
'Although it will be loud,
I'll dig his grave.'

Who'll be the parson?
'I,' quacked the duck,
'I'll use my good luck,
I'll be the parson.'

Who'll be the clerk?
'I,' shrieked the bat,
'I will wear my hat,
I'll be the clerk.'

Who'll be the link?
'I,' whispered the breeze,
Leaving a piece of cheese,
'I will be the link.'

Who'll be the chief mourner?
'I,' announced the sun,
Eating a bun,
'I'll be the chief mourner.'

Who'll carry the coffin?
'I,' bellowed the star,
'I will carry it on my car,
I'll carry the coffin.'

Who'll bear the pall?
'I,' cried the bark,
'As long as it's not in the dark,
I will bear the pall.'

Who'll sing a psalm?
'I,' hinted the rain,
'Although I will feel pain,
I'll sing a psalm.'

Who'll toll the bell?
'I,' laughed the ox,
'It will be like moving a cardboard box,
I will toll the bell.'

Travis Blake (10)
Sandringham Primary School

Who Killed The Shark?

(Based on 'Who Killed Cock Robin?' by Anon)

Who killed the shark?
'I,' said the jellyfish,
'With my electrifying swish,
I killed the shark.'

Who saw him die?
'I,' said the squid,
'While I undid my eyelid,
I saw him die.'

Who caught his blood?
'I,' said the seal,
'While I was having a scrumptious meal,
I caught his blood.'

Who'll make the shroud?
'I,' said the octopus,
'With my tentacles that are marvellous,
I'll make the shroud.'

Who'll dig the grave?
'I,' said the swordfish,
'With my shovel and magnificent dish,
I'll dig the grave.'

Who'll be the parson?
'I,' said the whale,
'With my trusty pail,
I'll be the parson.'

Who'll be the chief mourner?
'I,' said the eel,
'As I peel a meal,
I'll be the chief mourner.'

Who'll be the singer?
'I,' said the dolphin,
'As I swim out of a bin,
I'll be the singer.'

Who'll pull the coffin?
'I,' said the stingray,
'It will be like pulling hay,
I'll pull the coffin.'

Who'll pull the bell?
'I,' said the starfish,
'With a wish,
I'll pull the bell.'

Matthew Anelay (11)
Sandringham Primary School

Who Killed Daddy-Long-Legs?

(Based on 'Who Killed Cock Robin?' by Anon)

Who killed the daddy-long-legs?
'I,' said the praying mantis,
'With my bliss, but deadly, kiss,
I killed the daddy-long-legs.'

Who saw him die?
'I,' said the millipede,
'As I passed at my intense speed,
I saw him die.'

Who'll make the shroud?
'I,' said the spider,
'As I talk to the horse rider,
I'll make the shroud.'

Who'll catch the blood?
'I,' said the snail,
'But there is a horrible gale,
I'll catch the blood.'

Who'll dig the grave?
'I,' said the worm,
'But I'll have to have my perm,
I'll dig the grave.'

Who'll carry the coffin?
'I,' said the ladybird,
'While I do my crossword,
I'll carry the coffin.'

Who'll be the chief mourner?
'I,' said the slug,
'I'll cry on a rug,
I'll be the chief mourner.'

Who'll sing a psalm?
'I,' said the grasshopper,
'I'll fly over in my big chopper,
I'll sing a psalm.'

Who'll toll the bell?
'I,' said the caterpillar,
'I will, I'll play the guitar as well,
I'll toll the bell.'

All the bugs on Earth
Fell in sorrow
But none wanted to follow
Daddy-long-legs fell asleep on his pillow
And died a happy fellow.

Kayley Clark (11)
Sandringham Primary School

Who Killed The Shark?

(Based on 'Who Killed Cock Robin?' by Anon)

Who killed the shark?
'I,' said the jellyfish,
'With my little electric swish,
I killed the shark.'

Who saw him die?
'I,' said the squid,
'While I was building a pyramid,
I saw him die.'

Who caught his blood?
'I,' said the seal,
'While I was pushing a wheel,
I caught the blood.'

Who will make the shroud?
'I will make the shroud,' said the octopus,
'With my tentacles that are marvellous,
I will make the shroud.'

Who will dig the grave?
'I,' said the swordfish,
'With a big dish,
I will dig the grave.'

Who will be the parson?
'I,' said the whale,
'With a large tail,
I will be the parson.'

Who will be the chief mourner?
'I,' said the eel,
'As I eat my meal,
I will be the chief mourner.'

Who will be the singer?
'I,' said the dolphin,
'With a big sin,
I will be the singer.'

Who will carry the coffin?
'I,' said the stingray,
'With a pile of clay,
I will carry his coffin.'

Who will pull the bell?
'I,' said the starfish,
'With a big dish,
I will pull the bell.'

Amy Reckless (11)
Sandringham Primary School

Who Killed The Shark?

(Based on 'Who Killed Cock Robin?' by Anon)

Who killed the shark?
'I,' said the jellyfish,
'With my deadly swish,
I killed the shark.'

Who saw him die?
'I,' said the squid,
'While he hid,
I saw him die.'

Who caught his blood?
'I,' said the seal,
'With a truck wheel,
I caught his blood.'

Who will make the shroud?
'I,' said the octopus,
'Riding an underwater bus,
I will make the shroud.'

Who will dig his grave?
'I,' said the swordfish,
'With my dinner dish,
I will dig his grave.'

Who will be the parson?
'I,' said the whale,
'With a little hail,
I will be the parson.'

Who will be chief mourner?
'I,' said the eel,
'While I deliver a meal,
I will be chief mourner.'

Who will sing a song?
'I,' said the dolphin,
'With a sharp pin,
I will sing a song.'

Who will carry the coffin?
'I,' said the stingray,
'When I play away,
I will carry the coffin.'

Who will toll the bell?
'I,' said the starfish,
'With a tiny wish,
I will toll the bell.'

Rebecca Hutchings (10)
Sandringham Primary School

Who Killed Daddy-Long-Legs?

(Based on 'Who Killed Cock Robin?' by Anon)

Who killed daddy-long-legs?
'I,' said the praying mantis,
'As I blessed him with my bliss,
I killed the daddy-long-legs.'

Who saw him die?
'I,' said the millipede,
'As he started to bleed,
I saw him die.'

Who'll make the shroud?
'I,' said the spider,
'As I make it wider,
I'll make the shroud.'

Who'll catch the blood?
'I,' said the snail,
'As I cry and wail,
I'll catch the blood.'

Who'll dig the grave?
'I,' said the worm,
'With a wriggle and a squirm,
I'll dig the grave.'

Who'll carry the coffin?
'I,' said the ladybird,
'Not a mouse will be stirred,
I'll carry the coffin.'

Who'll be the chief mourner?
'I,' said the slug,
'As I give a long, deep shrug,
I'll be the chief mourner.'

All the bugs,
Cried and wailed,
As the birds glided in the wind
And the hail.

Laura Charnock (11)
Sandringham Primary School

Who Killed The Iguanodon?

(Based on 'Who Killed Cock Robin?' by Anon)

Who killed the iguanodon?
'I,' said the allosaurus,
'With my thesaurus,
I killed the iguanodon.'

Who saw him die?
'I,' said the diplodocus,
'With my focus,
I saw him die.'

Who caught his blood?
'I,' said the brachiosaurus,
'With my walrus,
I caught his blood.'

Who will make the shroud?
'I,' said T-rex,
'With my text,
I will make the shroud.'

Who will dig his grave?
'I,' said the stegosaurus,
'With the help of the brontosaurus,
I will dig his grave.'

Who will carry the coffin?
'I,' said the triceratops,
'Because I know that I will not drop,
I will carry the coffin.'

Who will sing the prayer?
'I,' said the velociraptor,
'Because I won the X Factor,
I will sing the prayer.'

Who will watch him be buried?
'We all will,' said the dinosaurs,
'With a round of applause,
We will watch him be buried.'

Tommy Taylor (11)
Sandringham Primary School

Young Writers Information

We hope you have enjoyed reading this book - and that you will continue to enjoy it in the coming years.

If you like reading and writing poetry drop us a line, or give us a call, and we'll send you a free information pack.

Alternatively if you would like to order further copies of this book or any of our other titles, then please give us a call or log onto our website at www.youngwriters.co.uk

**Young Writers Information
Remus House
Coltsfoot Drive
Peterborough
PE2 9JX**

(01733) 890066